Echoes of the

Events, People & Places in the 1970s in & around the Derbyshire Dales

Ron Duggins

Landmark Publishing

Published by

Ashbourne Hall, Cokayne Ave
Ashbourne, Derbyshire DE6 1EJ England
Tel: (01335) 347349 Fax: (01335) 347303
e-mail: landmark@clara.net
web site: www.landmarkpublishing.co.uk

ISBN 13: 978-1-84306-365-0

© Ron Duggins 2008

British Library Cataloguing in Publication Data: a catalogue record for this book is available from the British Library.

Printed by: Cromwell Press Ltd, Trowbridge
Designed by: Michelle Prost

Front Cover Top Left: A guard of honour on Smedley Street as the parade heads for the County Offices

Front Cover Bottom Left: In March 1979 this intrepid quintet of Matlock Town FC supporters set off from the town in a blizzard heading for Italy via Luton Airport. Various delays meant the group – Tom Oliver, John Lord, Roy Marchant, Tom Wright and Ian Cameron – arrived 23 hours later than expected, but still in time to see Matlock Town lose 2-1 to Pisa.

Front Cover Bottom Right: Rolf Harris brought his road show, Rolf's Walkabout, to Winster on a misty November day in 1979.

Front Cover Right: Rita Slack and her 20ft Sunflower.

Back Cover Top: Members of Youlgrave Junior Red Cross Group training under their leader Mrs Jan Wilson. They had been invited to take part in the 1971 Red Cross sports, which included tug of war, and Mrs Wilson, Bakewell Red Cross South Division Commander agreed to coach them.

Back cover Middle Left: Prince Charles 'unexpectedly' joined the High Peak Hunt soon after it left the Bull i' Thorn.

Back cover Middle Right: Members of Darley Dale Wanderers took on the ladies in a comic football match at the Whitworth Institute ground in June, 1976.

Back cover bottom: Happy Winster Dollies

Echoes of the Dales

Events, People & Places in the 1970s in & around the Derbyshire Dales

Ron Duggins

Dedication

*This book is dedicated to Ken Gregory who has always been
my inspiration. He is a remarkable man whose talent, patience,
kindness and generosity know no bounds.*

Landmark Publishing

Contents

ASHFORD

Ashford residents received a monster Christmas gift in December, 1979 – the opening of their new by-pass. Costing £600,000, the new road went round the outskirts of the picturesque village taking the pressure off the ancient bridges as well as making the narrow main street safer.

ASHOVER

Water was in short supply towards the end of 1970 for residents of Ashover and particularly on the Dovecotes Estate. Claims were made that taps were empty by 4 pm and unusable until the following morning. Residents were sharing washing facilities and getting their water from a storage tank.

Record entries and good weather set the seal for a great day out at the 1979 Ashover Show. Secretary Mons Haslam said they had sold all the 1000 programmes by noon and judges claimed higher standards in most classes. Pony class judges saw double when twins Julia and Gillian Gray (left) met up with twins Fleur and Philippa Hick.

Thirteen years old Julia and Gillian had ridden their ponies, Queen and Lady, from Matlock to the event, while eight-year-olds Fleur and Philippa (above) had come from nearby Amber Row.

Lifeguard Brian Dent was hailed as a hero after a nine-year-old almost died at Matlock Lido. Sally Easton, of Cromford, had been taking part in a Learn to Swim campaign in the learner pool and after she got out of the water it was thought she slipped, banged her head and fell into the water. Unconscious, she was spotted by a visitor who alerted Brian and between them they pulled Sally out and Brian immediately began resuscitation. Eventually she revived and was taken to Chesterfield Royal Hospital for an overnight stay.

BAKEWELL

Above: Twelve of the 30 players involved in the Derbyshire Grammar School XV v Derbyshire U21 XV fixture in November, 1971, were from the Ernest Bailey as Lady Manners Schools. Bill Edwards scored a try for the Schools and Robin Hooton for the U21s. Pictured are Richard Harris, Keith Lancaster, Stuart Watts, Tim Sargeant, Robin Hooton, Brian Cobb, Bill Gedye, Bill Edwards, John Hickmore, Peter Smith, Paul Riley and Alastair Munn.

Left: Red-headed Susan Moorby was crowned as the 1974 Bakewell Carnival Queen. The 15-year-old fourth-former at Lady Manners School was attended by Judith Raynes and Ruth Bradbury.

When James Hicks took to the road on his bike it was always something of a headache – whether to go one one wheel, two or even three. James (59) and a house furnisher, of Bakewell, said it took him only three weeks to master the unicycle and during that time he never fell off.

Top Right: Off for a spin on his bicycle.

Bottom Right: Leaning to the left as he guides the trike round a corner.

A three-day sponsored wheelchair push ended in pouring rain at Bakewell after having raised £1715 for Muscular Dystrophy Research. Ian and John Stoddart pushed their nephew Tony Stanbrook, of Great Longstone, from their home in Middlesbrough the 120 miles back to Derbyshire via Thirsk, York, Doncaster and Sheffield. Waiting to greet them was Bakewell's town mayor - Colonel Leslie Wright.

Happy Birthday sang Guides and Brownies from Bakewell as they celebrated their 60th anniversary and cut a cake at an entertainment in the Town Hall. Guider Mrs Valerie Reith presented Challenge Badges to Karen Patterson, Susie Grocock, Rachel Buchan, Vickie Hamilton, Sarah Price and Winnie Dwahliwal.

A "spring clean" in a Bakewell solicitors' office in 1978 led to forgotten treasures belonging to "The Lady with the Lamp" Florence Nightingale being unearthed. They were found in an old unlabelled deed box, which when opened, revealed notes, jewellery and other artefacts, which were believed to have been deposited at Bakewell in 1940 after the death of Mr Louis Shore-Nightingale, the last member of the family to live at Lea Hurst. Mr Michael Brooke-Taylor, Miss Cheryl Warren, Mrs Gillian Mawdsley and Miss Ruth Handley are pictured with some of the items.

Everybody loves Paris in the Spring goes the song – and it came true for Matthew Parris when he was elected MP for West Derbyshire in Spring 1979. The 29-year-old defeated Liberal candidate Peter Worboys and Labour's Bill Moore with an increased majority of 10,217.

BEELEY

Joanne Goodwin was crowned as Beeley's 1978 carnival queen by MP Matthew Parris. Her attendants were Carol Robinson and Katherine Turner with Kevin Tomlinson as page-boy.

Beeley Village Hall was the setting in 1974 for the pantomime Cinderella with Lesley Whetton (extreme left) playing the lead role. Pictured with her are Marlene Gilbert, Herbert Parker, Bob Cullimore, Heather Gilbert, Bernard Goodwin, Frank Robinson and Eddie Pratt.

A happy day for Lesley Whetton – pictured being crowned in 1974 as Beeley Carnival Queen by Mrs Liz Turner. Her attendants were Joanne Goodwin and Sara Rhodes with Andrew Nicholls as crown bearer.

BONSALL

Bonsall carnival Queen in 1974 was Gillian Astle, pictured here being crowned by Peter Swan.

Carrying on a family tradition in 1979, 15-year-old Norma Gratton became the fourth of seven sisters to be named as Bonsall Carnival Queen. Lynne (23), Beverley (21) and Jill (18) had been queens while the other sisters had been attendants.

After being trapped on a disused quarry ledge 85 feet above the ground, Rex a black labrador, was finally rescued by Matlock firemen. The animal had fallen 15 feet on to the ledge in Parish Quarry on the Via Gellia, and after the rescue Rex couldn't wait to give Fireman John Waller a grateful lick as colleagues Trevor Boulton and John Ireland carefully hold him.

The peaceful village of Bonsall was roused in 1978 when TV's Ted Moult arrived by stage coach and gave a blast from the past on a post-horn. He was there on a foggy day in December recording a BBC show that centred on Bonsall Cross. Caroline Dale from the Red House Stables supplied the coach, horses and post horn, while children from the village school performed "The Twelve Days of Christmas."

BRASSINGTON

Workmates joined together to say farewell to Mr Leslie Allsop after 50 years of working for Longcliffe Quarries at Brassington. He began work as a pony boy in 1928 but later became a charge hand in the stone grinding plant. A staunch supporter of Derby County FC he received a pair of binoculars from company chairman Mr Donald Shiel (left) and a cheque from Mr Bill Wilde (right) on behalf of his work colleagues.

CHATSWORTH PARK

Milkman Vaughan Taylor and his assistant George Ulyatt never let their customers down but the severe snowstorms in February 1979 almost spoiled their record. When the milk delivery lorry from Sheffield failed to get through to Matlock, the intrepid duo set out in their van to drive through a blizzard and collect their delivery from the dairy. They found the road through Chatsworth Park blocked and their mission had to be abandoned until the following day when an 85-mile round trip through Ripley and Chesterfield saw enough milk brought back to Matlock to keep customers happy for a few days.

The 1974 international Scout and Guide camp in Chatsworth Park saw thousands of youngsters enjoying themselves. This group from Matlock pose for Susan Beeston as she takes "one for the scrapbook". Also pictured among others are Kay Storey, Jill Vaines, Lesley Duggins, Laura Thomas and Christine Glover.

Spud-bashing Scouts Alistair Hook. Martin Greaves, Jonathan Crowder, Ralph Bates and Richard Maltby

CRICH

Above: An open landau carried Crich Carnival 'royalty from the Tramway Museum as they began a tour of the village. Mrs Winifred Hilton, crowned Queen Angela Wainwright who was accompanied by attendants Elizabeth Bowmer, Angela Martin, Jayne Boot and Kathryn Mason.

Left: Raymond Baxter, of the TV BBC1 programme Tomorrow's World, was at Crich Tramway Museum in 1971 filming a new series called Yesterday's World. He is pictured wrestling with the controls of a tram as he tries to avoid a very nasty accident.

CROMFORD

Above: Terrier Dinky nearly lost his life when a rabbit he was chasing led him into a water culvert where they were both trapped for several hours. Owned by Cromford butcher Don Kirk, Dinky was walking with a neighbour who slipped and let go of the lead. The dog spotted a rabbit and a chase began. The Fire Brigade were called and both Dinky and the rabbit were rescued.

Above: A third generation roof thatcher, George Mellor of Cromford never wanted to do anything else. His order book was generally full three years ahead even at £1,300 for a small cottage. It took two men ten hours to thatch 100 feet – known as a thatcher's square – at £85 per square, and a small cottage roof was generally twelve squares.

Left: Ambrosia rice pudding was among other tinned foods scattered over Cromford Hill after this out-of-control six-wheeler crashed head-on into a car travelling up the hill. The lorry driver was trapped in his cab with serious arm injuries and had to be cut free by Fire Service personnel. The car driver, from Tansley, received serious head injuries, while pedestrian Mrs Elizabeth Fern was treated for minor injuries after being knocked to the ground.

Mrs Winifred Hilton crowned Ann Barton (14) as Cromford Carnival Queen after her husband, Lord Lieutenant Colonel Peter Hilton, officially opened the event.

Below: Three years of restoration work by cub leader David Barnes led to the Cromford Pack having their very own bus which they used to get themselves and equipment to their first camp. David, of Stanton Lees, bought the 1961 AEC Reliance coach for £900 and spent hundreds of hours restoring it to pristine condition – he even re-built the massive 7.7 diesel engine. For its first outing the coach was sprayed in the Pack's colours of maroon and gold and at the rear was a panel bearing their full title.

Making hay while the sun shines – members of Matlock Round Table at their Mid-summer Fayre on Cromford Meadows brought along a wheelbarrow in which to carry home the proceeds that were earmarked for local charities and children's organisations.

Husband and wife hosts at the Bell Inn, Cromford, proved that they were a winning duo in front of the bar as well as behind it. In 1979 Reg and Margaret Wood were on target in the Wirksworth and District Darts and Dominoes League – Reg won the Landlords Knockout Trophy while Margaret won the Landladies Cup.

Unscheduled drama was played out on Cromford Meadows during the 1978 carnival. Jumpmaster of the Thunderbirds Parachute Team Geoff Poole jumped from 4,000 feet and only a split second after this picture was taken his 'chute momentarily collapsed at 80 feet. Luckily it re-inflated at 20 feet and he landed safely.

History came to life in 1971 when scholars and staff of Cromford CE School presented a pageant which told the story of the Arkwright era. Entitled "Lucky Thirteen" it was written and produced by teacher Miss Lowcock and every one of the 150 scholars took part.

Billy Mee, 70-year-old Cromford blacksmith, shows how it used to be in the old days when milk was delivered by horse and cart to the railway station from outlying farms. "On their way back the farmers would call in to have their horses re-shod, and pop over to The Greyhound for a jar or two while waiting. Many times it was fortunate the horses knew their own way home," he said. Bill ran the business for 50 years after he took it over from his father.

When youngster Rita Slack fed Plod the family cockatiel she occasionally put some of the sunflower seeds in her pocket for later use. The 10-year-old then planted the seeds in pots and when they began to grow transplanted them into the garden where some of them reached a height of 20 feet.

Cromford's 1979 Carnival was a huge success, raising over £1500 on the first day of the three-day celebrations. Queen of the Carnival was 16-year-old Paula Redfern who was crowned by Mrs Boot, whose husband Hamar officially opened the proceedings. Paula is pictured with her attendants.

As part of the Cromford Arkwight Festival in 1971, eighteenth century cricket was re-enacted on The Meadows. The Jedediah Strutt XI (captained by Colonel Peter Hilton) took on the Sir Richard Arkwright XI (captained by Alderman Bill Trippett). The Strutt team batted first and Ian Waite made 25 before being caught by footballer Eddie Shimwell. Les Bradbury made the highest score off one ball – 11 - and Tom Fletcher used a shovel instead of a bat. Colonel Hilton is pictured watching the umpire "spinning" the bat before the match that was watched by over 1000 spectators.

A cycling record was smashed in 1975 – 20 years after it was established by French ace Charles Lotre riding in the Tour of Britain in 1955, recording a time of 31 minutes 24 seconds for the 11-mile Cromford to Newhaven climb. In October 1975 three riders broke that time, Matlock Cycling Club's George Higton being the fastest in 27 mins 24 secs – an average speed of 22 mph. The other two riders were Terry Shaw (28.27) and John Herrett (31.23) both members of Belper Thorntons.

Cromford Football Club began their pre-season training earlier than usual in 1972 as they looked forward to tougher opposition in the Derbyshire Premier League. They also signed new players including Paul Heath and Kevin Widdowson from Tansley FC.

DARLEY DALE

Above: A 20-ton lorry loaded with limestone chippings crashed through a wall on the A6 at Darley Dale. A giant crane had to be used to retrieve it after the road had been closed most of the day.

Left: A euphonium player with over 50 years service in local bands finally hung up his instrument at the age of 62 – to make way for youngsters. Dyson Charlesworth, of Greenaway Lane, Darley Dale, began his working life as a nurseryman but later went on the railway as a guard. When the railway closed he joined the staff of the Bridges and Highways Department at the County Offices.

Hugh Walker Gregory began racing pigeons at the age of 10 and he was still racing them in 1972 at the age of 85. He began his working life as a joiner on the Stancliffe Estate at Darley Dale, later taking over the family market gardening business on Darley Hillside. He was a member of Darley Dale Homing Society, winning many trophies and races.

Carrots costing as much as £500 each were on sale at Darley Dale in 1971 making them the dearest in the world said Mr Herbert Hardy, founder of Direct Furnishing Supplies. He was speaking after magistrates fined him and his sons Ivan, Stuart and Keith for contravening the 1950 Shops Act by selling furniture on Sundays. Mr Hardy explained after the court case that as it was legal to buy carrots on Sunday his company would sell carrots and give away free furniture.

Quick thinking by Darley Dale builder Lewis Jackson probably saved the life of employee David Hall, of Matlock, when the side of a trench they were working in collapsed and a nearby lorry began to slide in on top of them. David was trapped by a concrete block so Mr Jackson scrambled clear and ran to a JCB digger which he used to wedge against the lorry and stop it crushing him. Dr James Macfarlane, Firemen Terry Robey, John Eccarius and Sub-Officer Jim Pearson are pictured stretchering the injured man from the scene.

Once a farmer always a farmer and even at the age of 90 Sam Wagstaffe still lent a hand running Holt Farm, Two Dales. Whether it was just keeping a watchful eye on the stock or sawing logs he said he had no intention of taking life easy.

Members of Darley Dale Wanderers took on the ladies in a comic football match at the Whitworth Institute ground in June, 1976. Even though they lost by 7 goals to 3, they could still raise a smile as they pocketed £43 for club funds.

Luckily no-one was injured when a stone-built store containing gas cylinders caught fire at the Two Dales Cara-Hols site in Darley Dale in the early hours. The alarm was raised at 2.15 am, the Fire Brigade summoned and caravanners moved to safety as flaming cylinders exploded and were thrown hundreds of yards. Partner Ivan Hardy said the company's first priority was the health and safety of visitors and he was thankful there were no injuries.

Everyone should have a Rolls Royce Shadow joked business man Len Marshall after he bought this gleaming masterpiece and set off for work from his home on the Via Gellia. Len, senior partner in Commercial Vehicle Dismantlers at Darley Dale, claimed he was later going to save up to buy a suit.

Sixteen-year-old Karen Spencer was chosen as Miss Whitworth 1978 and presented with the Goward Rose-bowl by Mrs Sheila Goward. Karen, of Two Dales, was a pupil at the Ernest Bailey Grammar School and the runner-up was Elaine Swindell, also of Two Dales.

In the 73 years he had been cycling, 80-year-old Denis Bradshaw's proud claim was that he never had one that was new. Mr Bradshaw, of Darley Dale, was a former train driver based in Rowsley Sidings, and he used his bicycle for work, pleasure and carrying equipment such as full watering cans to his allotment. "It's a grand way to get about," he said.

A brass-bound striking clock was presented to retired Head Teacher Joseph Hancock in 1978. The Head of Darley Dale County Primary School from 1932 to 1952, he was then appointed Head of Darley County Secondary School when it opened and until his retirement in 1964 after 40 years in teaching. Mr Hancock joined the National Union of Teachers in 1921 and held office until 1935, serving as secretary and later president of the Matlock association, president of the Derbyshire Association and secretary of the Retired Teachers Association. It was for this work that he received the clock from Mr Frank Turberville, chairman of the RTA, and he is pictured with Mrs Hancock and colleague Mr Douglas Brown.

Champagne - for both winners and losers - at the end of an unusual darts match at Darley Dale. Terry Dow claimed he could get a darts team made up from within his in-laws – the Prittys, and that they would challenge any local team with a similar make-up. The Bodens jumped at the chance to show off their prowess and the Church Inn, Darley Dale, was chosen as the venue. The Bodens clinched victory with a final double 20 and double 10.

Local government faced a new era in 1974 and members of West Derbyshire District Council were determined to drive a coach and horses – literally – through the old stuffy town hall image. They hired the Red House Stables coach and horses for a grand parade of council leaders through the district, starting at Chatsworth House from where the Duke and Duchess of Devonshire waved them off.

Collecting the coach and horses from the Red House Stables before going on to Chatsworth House are Councillor Terry Wray, Roy Bubb, Councillor Dennis Fisher and Coachman Ian Marriott.

Despite her age, eight years old Susan Bagshaw had that look of a very determined youngster. As the only girl taking part in the Matlock Mercury 1976 penalty-kick competition she spent all her spare time practising in readiness for the event.

ELTON

Elton Women's Institute members celebrated their 25th anniversary in 1976 with a dinner at the Newhaven Hotel. Thirty-four ladies were present including Mrs Mary Turner (centre, middle row) who was their first president.

In the swim at Matlock Lido are Elton mothers and toddlers under the supervision of village school Headmistress Heather Swindell who hit upon the idea of bringing them along with the juniors to their weekly sessions.

Lea & Holloway

Above: A family link of 74 years was broken when Miss Anne Jones retired from Holloway Post Office in 1975. Her father Edward moved from Wales and took over the business in 1901 and she became sub-postmistress in 1954

Right: Striking firemen and Royal Air Force personnel worked side-by-side in January 1978 to contain a fire at the old Co-op Store in Holloway. Matlock firemen remained on-call during the strike and three full-time and one retainer went to the incident when the alarm was raised in the early evening. The building was well alight by the time two Green Goddess crews arrived from Chesterfield, and it was midnight before the fire was extinguished, only for the Matlock crew to be recalled three hours later when the blaze broke out again.

Lea and Holloway carnival was graced by the presence of the Duke of Devonshire when he opened the proceedings by crowning 11-year-old Catherine Brown as queen, with Gordon Thorpe as her king. The day's events raised over £600 for local charities.

Five members of the Lea and Holloway Girl Guide Group received their Queen's Guide Awards in 1978 from District Commissioner Mrs Betty Watson. Left to right are Lucinda Holmes, Ellen Ravensdale, Kaye Bearpark, Ruth Allen, Anne Thoday and Mrs Watson.

When Susan Foster was one year old she won the Most Beautiful Baby award at Dethick, Lea and Holloway's annual carnival. Exactly ten years later here she is (top left) - Queen of the Carnival, alongside her King Paul Bowmer, and their courtiers.

GREAT LONGSTONE

Champions of the Longstone Cricket League at the end of the 1978 season were Longstone CC and pictured admiring the trophy are captain Peter Shimwell, president Roy Finney and team members.

MATLOCK

Neatly dressed junior scholars of All Saints' School, Matlock, pose for the camera at their Speech Day held at Sherwood Hall in 1970. Among them are Neil Johnson, Charlie Davies, Alison Loxton, Lesley Duggins, Gill Henshaw, Simon Croft, Jennifer Channon, Simon Kreibich and Laura Thomas.

Referee George Sellers (left) keeps a keen eye on Ian Flint as he releases the bowl in a Matlock Bowls Club tournament on the Hall Leys Park. On the right is team mate David Goodier.

Three baby woodpeckers were found in a tree that had been brought from Shrewsbury to Derbyshire prior to being cut up. They were rescued and taken to Mr and Mrs Eric Bradshaw's bird sanctuary on Matlock Green. Unfortunately one died but Mr Bradshaw is pictured here busily feeding one of the two survivors.

The military funeral took place at Matlock in 1972 of Private Michael Prime who died in an IRA ambush in Belfast. His wife Joyce and he had been married two years, he had been in the Royal Army Pay Corps eleven months and in Ireland only three weeks. His family home was at Mettesford, Matlock, from where the cortege left on its journey to St Giles Parish Church.

A large gathering of mourners stood in St Giles Churchyard to pay their final tribute as Private Michael Prime was slowly lowered by his military colleagues into his final resting place.

After several years of campaigning and fund-raising to "Raise the Roof" work began on the demolition of the high diving boards at Matlock Lido outdoor swimming pool.

Tilers at work on the pool's new base.

Scaffold in place as the roof takes shape.

After months of closure Matlock Lido re-opened in 1972. The diving boards had gone, the concrete base replaced, changing rooms altered and more importantly it had a roof.

"The best in the world" was how Sybille Chapman described her husband Walter as she presented him with a special gift in 1972. They were celebrating their 25th wedding anniversary and the gift was a new Mercedes that had been secretly delivered to their home at the Crown Hotel in Matlock.

At the age of 84 Mrs Florrie Daniels showed how a high kick should be done to fellow residents of Dene Court in Matlock. It was all part of a gentle keep-fit programme aimed at keeping pensioners supple and also an aid to co-ordination and balance.

Trainee journalist Wendy Higton was swept off her feet by a Japanese unicyclist when he called in to the Matlock Mercury office on Bakewell Road. Takafumi Ogasawara left his home town of Matsumoto in 1970 on a round-the-world trip and after visiting Libya, Egypt, the USA, Canada, Mexico, Brazil, Honduras, Israel and many other countries finally arrived in Matlock in July 1972.

Matlock Band under conductor Murray Slater hit a high note when they came away with third prize in the National Band Finals in 1972. The previous year they were seventh, but this time the adjudicators spoke of "a good sense of music-making behind the direction".

Maurice Webb takes eight of his eleven dogs for a walk from his home at Lea Bridge. The ten Irish setters and one springer spaniel were no trouble - only expensive to feed even by 1974 standards. Mr Webb, secretary of the Matlock and District Canine Society, and his wife were members of a group which specialised in finding homes for abandoned Irish setters.

Four Matlock girls had a terrifying experience when they went to see David Cassidy at the White City Stadium in London. They were part of an audience of 38,000 young fans all eager to see and hear their idol. As the concert began the crowd pushed towards the stage crushing those at the front. Cassidy left the stage after ten minutes while order was restored, returning later. On their way to the Stadium – the girls, Karen Smith, Jackie Fentem, Susan Deacon and Jayne Boden - were caught up in the crush to get to Shepherds Bush underground station. Karen said "It was chaos. I thought we were going to be suffocated. It was terrifying." Safely back home they proudly showed off a giant picture of David.

Award winning Matlock Choir are pictured here in 1976 with their conductor Mrs Gloria Hollingworth, daughter of previous conductor Harold D Wildgoose and grand-daughter of Lubin G Wildgoose, who founded the choir in 1901. Those pictured include Margaret Fearn, Monica Wall, Sheila Taylor, Cynthia Hollins, Jean Brannigan, Marjorie Wardman, Cynthia Wright, Phyllis Slater, Doreen Moreton, Diane Wildgoose, Audrey Briddon, Hilda Farnsworth, Margaret Kent, Audrey Wildgoose, Ida Greatorex, Ann Wall, Vera Wright, Ida Palfreyman, John Wall, Ernest Farnsworth, Aubrey Bearpark, Ray Twyford, Desmond Charleson, Les Frost and Peter Carley.

A 12-year-old boy who fell down a disused mine shaft on Masson Hillside is pictured being rescued by Fire Service, Police and Ambulance personnel. Andrew Peat from Nottingham plunged 80 feet down the shaft after he had strayed into a privately-owned field. Leading the rescue was Station Officer Tony Allen, and pulling Andrew to the surface are Firemen John Waller, Bill Hodkin, Mick Allen, Arthur Parks and John Eccarius and Ambulancemen Ted Widdeson and Bert Thomas.

After a series of disasters and near-disasters over the years involving people and animals falling into open mineshafts in the county, work finally began on capping the estimated 2,300. The Peak District Mines Historical Society in conjunction with Derbyshire County Council began the task on the same shaft from which the young boy (above) was rescued in April, 1974.

Below: A bite from a hamster named Hercules left Peter Bell with a bleeding finger and a trip to hospital. Peter, co-director and curator of Riber Fauna Reserve, had four stitches in the wound.

Above: Workers digging a trench to lay a new gas main on Bank Road in Matlock were surprised to find a row of metal stanchions which, on examination, proved to be the ones which held the cable bogies of the old Bank Road Tramway.

Celebrating their Golden Jubilee with this picture in 1978 were the Old Bailean 1st XV. Back row (left to right): John Packard, Ron Marquand, Robin Gray, Steve Andrews, Graham French, Ian Nicholson, Keith Lancaster, Len Haywood, Eric Phipps and David Gray; (front) Barry Wood, Dave Ross, John Burden, Pete Rooney, Chris Loeber, Alan Lambe and Chris Roome.

This quartet of Matlock Cycling Club riders were all prize winners at the Club's open Riber Hill climb in 1978. Mark Hughes (second left) was fastest schoolboy in 6 mins 4.6 seconds; George Higton 4th overall with 5 31.1, John Bennett 1st veteran with 6 26.6 and Andrew Gaskell (extreme left) received the prize for being last.

Matlock's "hello" girls said "goodbye" when their telephone plugs were finally pulled at the New Street Exchange in 1978. Supervisor Mrs Betty Kirkland had clocked up nearly 27 years service and admitted it was a sad day as the switchboard closed and subscribers were transferred to Derby.

A wall-board containing all the names of former county council chairmen was unveiled at the County Offices in December 1978. Pictured (left to right) are the widows of former chairmen George Cocker (1974) and Jock Anderson (1965), Alderman Norman Wilson (1967 and 1978), Alderman Norman Gratton (1962-1965), Alderman Mrs Gladys Buxton (1957-1962), Alderman Bill Trippett (1964-1973) and Councillor George Coleman (1975).

Matlock licensee John Wright was banned from exercising his Doberman dog around the perimeter of Causeway Lane Football Club ground so he retaliated by banning club officials and supporters from his car park at the Railway Hotel. The Club put up notices banning dog walking – John bought paint and a brush and wrote his own sign banning shoppers and gamblers. Shoppers used his Brewery-owned car park while shopping in town and "gamblers" who used it while visiting the Supporters Auxiliary office there.

A party of 49 Scouts, Leaders and their wives pictured on Matlock Station as they set off for two weeks in Germany. Darley Dale and Matlock All Saints Groups were meeting their counterparts in Coburg for 14 days of cultural learning. For their part the British Group had been learning the complicated steps of morris dancing from the Winster Morris Men.

Ready for the off is Dudley Johnson on his 1911 Triumph motorcycle at the start of a 100-mile journey. He was raising funds for the North East Derbyshire Scanner Fund and 1600 people had entered a competition to guess how long the trip would take him. Starting and finishing outside C Farmer Ltd's shop on Causeway Lane, the route was two laps of a circuit that went through Cromford, Newhaven, Brierlow Bar, Taddington, and Bakewell and the time was 4 hours 43 minutes and 50 seconds. Starting the event was Mr Herbert Hardy, of DFS, and Mr Charles Farmer donated a digital clock radio to the competition winner.

Always a bit of a wag, collie Dusky Williams got into the party spirit at Matlock Dog Training Club's festive party. Wearing a sparkling hat and with a squeaker firmly in her mouth she could hardly wait for the real fun to begin.

Building up steam for a stately trip along the river bank in Matlock is Cyril Swain's "Flying Scotsman". Every year hundreds of youngsters made the quarter-mile return journey on Sundays and Bank Holidays, but the rest of the week was serviced by a diesel loco. Mr Swain and his wife Rosa were very proud of the fact that despite inflation rises their fare had remained at 10p for the past three years.

Opened in 1935 to commemorate King George's Silver Jubilee, the boating lake on the Hall Leys Park in Matlock used paddle boats before the introduction on petrol boats. Mr Jim Garthwaite and Mr Cyril Swain had both been responsible for the boats popularity over the years, and here is Martin Garthwaite carrying on the tradition.

When Matlock's only well dressing was vandalised for the second year running parents of the dressers mounted a night-long guard to protect it. Built by the All Saints Brownie Pack and erected at the side of the Dimple Spa Well it raised £65 for Mencap.

Matlock schoolboy Richard Allen was hailed a hero after he rescued a 12-year-old girl from the sea off the Cornwall coast while on holiday with his parents, Geoff and Anne. Richard (15) was out in a tiny plastic dinghy when he spotted the girl in difficulties in her dinghy. She had lost both oars and was being driven by strong winds towards rocks, he eventually reached her and towed her to a ledge where they waited until help arrived.

Cadbury's "Learn to Swim" campaign at Matlock Lido was a huge success. The four-week programme was scheduled to accommodate 150 children, but in the end 900 passed through the instructors hands. Pool Superintendent Jack Soppitt arranged two back-up courses that kept the six instructors at full stretch. Mr Soppitt, instructors and some of the children are pictured with their Cadbury certificates.

Below: George Hubbard – the big man with the big beard - that was how he was known in the district. However, few people knew that behind the beard was a man who survived Dunkirk, managed to reach St Nazaire to board the troopship Lancastria, which was sunk as it left the harbour. He was eventually plucked from the sea by a Chinese ship and returned to England where he was transferred to the RAMC based in Birmingham. He vividly recalled the Coventry bombings and the horrors he saw and the six babies he delivered there while in the back of ambulances. He once delivered one in the waiting room on Matlock Station. George was an ardent worker in the St John Ambulance Brigade as well as being trainer with Matlock Town Football Club.

Above: Plenty to smile about – trombonist Jane Greensmith (Fred to her friends) had just won best solo performance at Buxton Brass Band Entertainment contest. As a member of Matlock Band she was also with the musicians who took the Premier Trophy with 189 points out of a possible 200.

Left: Heading down to the river...Julie Lea (15) couldn't wait to get in some more angling practice. After only 13 months experience, the John Turner School pupil from Matlock was already beating the men at their own game. In her first match she came second, but in the next event she was outright winner, weighing in 3lb 6oz with 14 fish - and her catch was heavier than all the other competitors put together.

Life can sometimes be difficult for identical twins, but imagine a referee's problems when they play football in the same team. David and Barry Shaw – aged 25 - played for Woodland Wanderers in the 1979 season and were often mistaken for each other, particularly if conditions were muddy. After one particular match, Barry was given rave reviews in the Press despite him being ill in bed at the time while in another game David scored but Barry was given the credit.

Wearing a casual jumper and burgundy-coloured trousers tucked into knee-length shiny boots, 18 years old Patricia Walker went to her former school's speech day to collect her A-level certificate and House captain's prize. But she was confronted by her former Senior Mistress at the Ernest Bailey Grammar School, Miss D M Hart, who told her she could not go on stage dressed like that. Patricia, who had made the trip from college in Salford, had a hasty discussion with her parents and went back to her home in Matlock and returned in her old school outfit of sweater, grey skirt, white stockings and flat shoes.

The magnificence of the Cinema House in Matlock with its single screen is illustrated by these two pictures: one taken from the rear of the balcony with its double seats and looking towards the screen; the other taken from the screen looking towards the upper balcony, with seating below forming a lower balcony. 'Pop' stars performed at the Cinema, Matlock Operatic Society's annual offerings attracted full houses, as did professional boxing and wrestling matches and school speech days. But in the early seventies everything changed: it became The Ritz with three screens, gaudy fluorescent signs and eventually a bingo hall was added. The "What's on" hoarding is pictured being hauled into place above the entrance vestibule where it hung for the next 30 years.

Happy bingo players outside the Matlock Ritz waiting for transport to take them to the Pancake Derby at the Sheffield Ritz. They took part in pancake races and, of course, played the odd game of bingo. Included in this picture are Christine Holt, Margaret Gregory, Sheila Newborough, Bridget White, Rose Fisher, Lily Rouse, Enid Ward, Lucy Wilson Duggins, Carol Bent, Kathy West and Connie Palmer.

For the second time in 14 months, residents of Lime Tree Road in Matlock had a miracle escape from disaster. April, 1978, saw a 16-ton articulated vehicle out of control and loaded with a 14-ton excavator hurtling down the steep hill. Immediately before the Hurst Farm junction the whole outfit overturned, demolishing walls and scattering debris over a wide area but luckily no homes were damaged. The only injury received was to the driver who suffered cuts and bruises.

Within a few weeks of the 1979 season opening the Old Baileans Hockey Club 1st team had won two tournaments. Pictured are (back row) Jackie Cachart, Sue Britland, Chris Bust, Philippa Cooper, Phyllis Billam, Kate Pheasey, Anita Gregory and umpire Peter Greaves; (front row) Jane Whitworth, Jill Gratton, Angela Hooton, Laura Thomas and Sue May.

Winning smiles from Matlock Post Office employees Brian Boam and Ian Flint after they had won the Midland Regional Post Office Crown Green Bowls Doubles championship. The last three rounds were played in pouring rain and on a green that had in places two inches of standing water.

They say its quicker by coach – even stage coach in this case. An overturned lorry almost blocked the A6 at Hooley's Estate, but it didn't stop the mail getting through. The Red House stage coach team took the hazard in their stride and continued on their way.

For newly-weds Lyn and David Carter the pitter-patter of tiny feet could only mean one thing – Rupert was hungry. A seven-week old racoon, Rupert had to be fed every four hours and the couple took it in turn to do the honours. The mother racoon had produced four youngsters but was finding it difficult to cope with them all so Lyn, an animal keeper at Riber Wildlife Park, volunteered to "adopt" Rupert. Every morning he was taken in a shopping basket back to Riber and at the end of the day made the return journey back to Lyn and David's home on Matlock Bank.

Come rain, hail or even snow nothing can stop a true football fan following his team. In March 1979 this intrepid quintet of Matlock Town FC supporters set off from the town in a blizzard heading for Italy via Luton Airport. Various delays meant the group – Tom Oliver, John Lord, Roy Marchant, Tom Wright and Ian Cameron – arrived 23 hours later than expected, but still in time to see Matlock Town lose 2-1 to Pisa.

Card-playing Mollie Wragg often used to call in to Matlock Conservative Club for a game of whist – that is until club officials banned her after the 1974 general election. Labour supporter Mollie was at the Town Hall when James Scott-Hopkins was re-elected MP for West Derbyshire and when the result was announced she called out "Come in Morning Cloud, your time is up", referring to Ted Heath and his yacht. "I thought he was spending too much time on it and not enough time running the country in a time of crisis," she said.

Below: The Fire Service occasionally are called out to incidents of a less serious nature – and this was one of them. Stephen Calladine, a student at Matlock College of Education's Rockside Hall found he was snookered even before he began a game pool. A 10p coin, which was to be used in the automatic slot, fell into a corner pocket and when Stephen tried to retrieve it found he was well and truly stuck. His friends struggled for 20 minutes to release him before calling Matlock Fire officers Leading Fireman Roy Blair and Fireman John Waller who took off the outer part of the table and released him - but not the money.

Armed raiders got away with almost £10,000 from the Midland Bank in May 1970. When staff went to open the strong room at the Dale Road premises they were confronted by two hooded men who ordered cashier Michel Swan to "Open it up" before he was knocked unconscious with a crowbar. Senior cashier Jeffrey Cook had a shotgun poked into his ribs as he unlocked the doors but he was unharmed as was a woman cashier. The thieves were believed to have entered the Bank by sawing through bars on a small window close to the river bank and also making their escape through the same way. Mr Swan later needed eight stitches to a head wound.

An empty office block adjoining the Williams Deacon's Bank was struck by lightning on the day before the robbery at the Midland Bank – only yards away. No-one was injured but the damage was estimated at many thousands of pounds. The fire brigade were called to make the building safe and remove debris.

Struggling through the snow in 1979, is 14-year-old Elizabeth (Libby) Statham. Schools were closed and it was difficult getting about, so she used her time helping her parents deliver milk in the family business.

Metal detecting was all the rage in the 1970s, and the Matlock area had its own club called PAST (Peak Artifacts Search Team). Leading lights were David Skinner (secretary) and founder member Doug Goodall who is pictured with his metal detector.

Only 23 people turned out for a 20-mile sponsored walk to raise money in 1976 for Matlock Town Football Club – but they still raised £520. Club chairman Cliff Britland took part as did the youngest supporter Diane West. Trainer George Wragg is pictured cooling down the hot feet of Michael Haywood, Andrew Stevenson, Leon Stone, David Apperley. Graham Langley, John Apperley and Tim Oliver.

Visitors to Matlock on Saturday, April 26, 1975, could have been forgiven for thinking they were in a ghost town...shops were closed and the streets almost deserted. Yes, that was the day Matlock Town Football Club and thousands of supporters were at Wembley Stadium to witness what will be remembered for many years to come: Matlock Town versus Scarborough in the FA Trophy Final. The Seasiders were always favourites to win, having won it previously, but this time it was not to be and the Gladiators' 4-0 victory meant the Trophy headed to Derbyshire. There were amazing scenes of jubilation at Wembley and during the parade and reception at the County Offices on the team's return and these are just a few of the dozens of "snapshots" taken that weekend.

Ready for Wembley - supporters wait patiently on Matlock Station for their big day out

Peter Swan and the team's mascot arrive at Wembley

Above: A friendly chat between the two captains as the teams nervously wait

Left: Colin Oxley (left) slots in Matlock's first goal

Below: Jubilation from his team-mates as Colin Dawson makes it 2-0

Tom Fenoughty's free kick hits the back of the net and it's 3-0

Nick Fenoughty (right) leaves the 'keeper stranded for the fourth goal

Jubilant Tom Fenoughty raises the FA Trophy high
above his head

Excitement among Matlock supporters as they realise the Trophy is theirs

The 'Gladiators' make their way back down to the pitch with their trophies

Colin Dawson makes the most of the day

A guard of honour on Smedley Street as the parade heads for the County Offices

Adulation from the hundreds as they greet their heroes at the County Offices

Peter Swan looks on as Colin Oxley ad-dresses the crowds

MATLOCK BATH

Under this overturned 32-ton articulated vehicle is a flattened telephone kiosk. Owned by Tarmac Derby Ltd, the lorry was carrying 16 tons of gravel that was spilled on to the Promenade at Matlock Bath, after crushing the kiosk, iron gates and railings. The driver from Codnor received lacerations and concussion. The kiosk was later re-sited.

Matlock Bath RSPCA volunteer Mrs Joyce George turned her home and gardens into a refuge for all sorts of birds and animals. Injured swans, dogs, cats and even goldfish received her devotion, but when she was given three baby squirrels she certainly had her hands full. She is seen giving one of them the hourly feeds that they needed.

Comedian Dave Allen casts a wary eye over a lobster that was presented to him before a meal at the New Bath Hotel in Matlock Bath. Having already lost part of a finger he was not too keen to lose another.

Julie Goodyear – Bett Lynch of TVs Coronation Street – switched on Matlock Bath's 1972 Illuminations after travelling from Matlock in a horse-drawn landau accompanied by her son. She was taken to the Bandstand where she took over the baton as Bakewell Band played "Lily the Pink." After signing autographs she joined her family on a riverside tour of the £8,000 Illuminations.

When TV personality Wendy Craig switched on the 1974 Illuminations at Matlock Bath they went on with a bang. As she pulled the giant lever to start the celebrations, the control panel collapsed and coloured balloons floated gently up into the still-dark night sky. At the second attempt all went well and over 4000 visitors enjoyed the bigger and better lights.

After all the switch-on hilarity Wendy signed hundreds of autographs and, as tradition dictated, conducted Bakewell Silver Band.

Newsboy Simon Kreibich (14) of Matlock Bath won £25 as a runner-up in the North/North West region for his entry in the W H Smith 1975 Sports Awards. The competition was open to all newsboys and girls employed by newsagents supplied by Smiths. Simon had been delivering papers for Matlock Bath newsagent Tom Lound for two years and was a pupil at the Ernest Bailey Grammar School.

Huge diggers moved into the River Derwent at Artists' Corner in the summer of 1978 at the start of Severn-Trent's long-awaited flood protection scheme for Matlock. The plan was to excavate the river bed and give it more depth over a 600-metre stretch down stream and remove the first weir in a scheme costing around half a million pounds.

Parking in Matlock has always been a problem, but occupants of cottages below St John's Road took exception at where this lorry was left. Luckily no-one was injured when the vehicle plunged 30 feet and came to rest on its side high above Dale Road near Artists Corner. It was eventually lifted clear later the same night.

Three "Swiss Misses" handed out souvenirs to visitors as they arrived on the first train in seven years to stop at Matlock Bath. The girls were Ruth Wood (14), Maria Adams (12) and Carol Oliver (15) and they joined civic leaders to welcome the 200 people who had paid £1.40 for the day trip from London to Matlock Bath.

Sitting among the daffodils in Whitworth Park is 17-year-old Carol Oliver, 1973 Miss Whitworth. Carol, of Holme Road, Matlock Bath, was a shorthand typist with Ivonbrook Quarries.

Derby County and England footballer Alan Hinton pictured crowning Winster's Olga Terenczyn as the 1971 Miss Derbyshire.

Coronation Street came to Matlock Bath in 1971 in the shape of Stan Ogden who chose to give the Rover's Return a miss in favour of switching on the Illuminations. He was accompanied by his ballet dancer wife Penny. Pictured with Stan, in real life Bernard Youens, is the "Man in the White Suit" Councillor Remo Tinti, who had been commentator at the Lights for 18 years until he resigned in 1968. Mr Tinti was invited back to join the festivities which were begun 80 years previously.

MIDDLETON BY WIRKSWORTH

Hands reach out to help an injured Nottingham woman as she was lifted out of a disused mine shaft on Middleton Moor in 1974. She had become separated from her husband while collecting moss for wreath-making and fell down the overgrown open shaft. Her husband searched for her, but only when he noticed a scarf entangled in a shrub above the shaft did he realise his wife's plight. Police, fire, ambulance and cave rescue personnel arrived and eventually the woman was brought out alive and air-lifted by helicopter to hospital.

The injured woman's husband holds her arm as she was placed on a stretcher.

A young man with high expectations – that was 17-year-old Tony Cachart, of Middleton-by-Wirksworth. The apprentice electrician in 1972, was one of 20 members of the Titanic Salvage Company which had been promised £2-million worth of backing for the attempt to raise the wreck of the Titanic which lay in three miles of water off Newfoundland. Looking ahead, Tony had his eyes set on other projects such as salvaging HMS Hood, the German warship Graf Spee and the burned-out Queen Elizabeth in Hong Kong harbour.

Two couples from Middleton by Wirksworth are pictured after completing the arduous 270-mile Pennine Walk in 1978. Relaxing outside the Rising Sun and re-living the journey from Edale to Kirk Yetholme are Teresa and Joe Sparham and Ann and Steve Green.

NEWHAVEN

Acting as leader of the pack in January 1978 was Prince Charles. He 'unexpectedly' joined the High Peak Hunt soon after it left the Bull i' Thorn where members had enjoyed a traditional stirrup cup. The Prince, who had driven to Hindlow in his green Range Rover, wore a blue jacket trimmed with red.

PILSLEY

The Marchioness of Hartington, accompanied by her husband the Marquis, crowned Jill Wedderspoon (12) as Pilsley village queen in 1970. Attendants were Tracey Bonsall (6) and Elizabeth Aris (6) with Robert Hill as crown bearer. It was also Robert Barnes (7) lucky day – he won a ham by winning the bowling for a pig contest as well as the treasure hunt.

When Elizabeth Aris was crowned Pilsley carnival queen in 1979 she became Queen Elizabeth II, having previously held that position in 1975. With a population of only 150 there was a scarcity of eligible girls, so it was a matter of sharing the honour among three older ones – in fact the retiring queen was Dorothy, Elizabeth's elder sister.

Mr and Mrs Hugo Read were guests of honour at the 1971 Pilsley Fair when comic football and tug of war were on the programme. Mrs Read judged the fancy dress and Mr Read crowned Wendy Bonsall (14) as Queen. They are pictured with attendants Susan Heathcote and Elizabeth Miles. The theme of the well dressing was "The Good Samaritan" and although it was delayed in being erected it was judged to be the best ever.

ROWSLEY

The end of the line as workmen put the last blocks in place to seal the Haddon Tunnel and finally close the main rail route to Manchester.

Above: A gardener who specialised in sweet peas and who went to work temporarily at Rowsley's Peacock Hotel was still there in 1976 – 36 years later. At that year's Chelsea Flower Show John McPhee showed eleven different varieties of sweet pea and 700 blooms altogether and was awarded the Silver Medal. He also developed a new variety called Marie Marshall, named after his eldest grand-daughter.

Right: When you are over six feet tall it is so easy to block people's view, but Derbyshire Times photographer Ken Gregory was always happy to oblige others by crouching down. Here he is in action getting the low-down on the Church Lane well dressing at Rowsley's Festival. Entitled "Bless the Children" it was designed and built by a team organised by Mrs Dorothy Wells.

A bench full of memories for these railway men who clocked up 244 years' service between them. All from Rowsley, they are Jesse Froggatt (76), a former goods guard for 48 years; Bill Bailey (72) former signalman 49 years; Alf Hancock (83), former wagon wheel tapper 52 years; Roland Pope (79) former goods guard 48 years; and Arthur Marsh (71), former engine driver 47 years.

STARKHOLMES

Former MP for West Derbyshire, James Scott-Hopkins, opened the 1979 Starkholmes Gala Day which raised over £750. Later he crowned Gwyneth Holland as Gala Queen.

TANSLEY

Landlord Albert Fletcher of the Plough Inn, Two Dales, always dreamed of moving with his family to a new home when he retired. When some of the pub's regulars heard about it they suggested they could help get the project under way and for weeks they used their spare time digging foundations, preparing floors and putting the services in. The only payment they had was refreshments delivered to the site in a field at Tansley. Pictured with Albert are his daughter Carol, Neil Ashcroft, David Ollerenshaw, Peter Walker and Howard Walters.

When Tansley newsagent Freddie Webster was taken into hospital he thought he would have to close his shop – but good neighbours Mrs Mary Neville (left) and Mrs Rosemary Mantell thought otherwise. They kept the shop open and the business running – even on Sundays – serving the villagers as Fred had done for many years.

Twice Penny Bartlett won the Junior Open Jumping event at Ashover Show but never received the trophy for the feat. Apparently it had not been seen for two years, so show organisers decided that rather than the 15-year-old go home to Tansley empty-handed they loaned her a trophy. No wonder Leighton Edgar is taking a close look – it was for the best Ayrshire heifer in calf.

Penny's mother Yvonne ('Dickie') owned the successful Tansley Riding School and had many horses and ponies - but her favourite was called 'Bandit'. He had been sent to a nearby farm to be destroyed, Dickie heard about it and promptly bought him. He became a firm favourite with dozens of riders...and as one youngster said "He's the most gentle pony I have ever ridden." Mrs Bartlett was for many years a conductress with the North Western Road Car Company, an accomplished table tennis player and a formidable bridge player.

Retired schoolteacher Mrs Dorothy Barber opened the 1971 Tansley Field Day when many of her former pupils were there to renew acquaintances. She is pictured with Miss Tansley Janice Whysall and attendants Karen Cooper and Tracy Yates.

Charles White School pupil Lorna Cross (15) was crowned as Miss Tansley 1979 by her predecessor Claire Wilson, and the annual Field Day was opened by Mr John Hall, former Head of Tansley Junior School.

New signings Charlie Cresswell and Graham Jamieson joined Tansley FC's new trainer Brian Ashbrook for the start of the 1972 season. Team manager Reg Whitworth said they would continue to play in the B Section of the Sutton and Skegby League on Saturdays and that they had been accepted into Division 2 of the Chesterfield Sunday League.

TIDESWELL

Climax to the 1979 Tideswell Wakes and Well Dressings week was the carnival procession. Methodist Rose Queen Sharron Hallam and her attendants gave happy smiles and waves to the hundreds of visitors as they passed by.

A saucy French Connection entertained and had their collecting boxes at the ready.

There were 18 entrants in the 1979 Miss Derbyshire contest at Matlock Bath Pavilion - but there was only one winner - Amanda Simmonite. Amanda, from Tideswell, and a pupil at Lady Manners School in Bakewell, was crowned by Bob Taylor, Derbyshire and England wicket-keeper. Amanda is pictured with runner-up Karen Morris (left) and retiring Miss Derbyshire Jacqui O'Brien.

Two Dales

A giant reel of paper weighing 1.5 tonnes was hurled down Sydnope Hill, Two Dales, when the lorry carrying it crashed. Householders were shocked when they realised the "missile" was wedged only feet from the side of their property. Mrs Barbara Pyatt said that although the accident was higher up the hill she heard the same terrific bang that she had heard many times before. "I ran to the phone to alert the emergency services and seconds later I was conscious of another bang," she said. "It was only when I went into the kitchen and looked through the window that I realised what a narrow escape we all had." Pictured near the paper reel are Mrs Pyatt, her mother Mrs Gwen Watts and neighbour Mrs Jean Webster.

WINSTER

Only three miles to go... Walter Terenczyn pauses for breath before his final assault on the hills leading up to his home in Winster after walking barefoot all the way from Manchester. His marathon effort was to raise funds towards the provision of a children's playing field.

Winster's carnival queen in 1979 was 10-year-old Helen Wirham, pictured here with attendants Bridget Concannon and Michelle Hopkinson.

Happy Winster Dollies - Louise Hopley, Mary Witham and Margaret Hopley

Winster's Morris Men proved their popularity when they danced in the village Main Street during the carnival in 1979, following on from their debut the previous year when they re-formed after 20 years. Helen Witham (aged 10) was Carnival Princess.

Rolf Harris brought his road show, Rolf's Walkabout, to Winster on a misty November day in 1979. He spent the first half-hour signing autographs and later visited the school where he entertained children with his songs and drawings. He even drew a self-portrait in the grime on the side of his tour bus.

Sir David and Lady Huddie were guests of Winster Carnival Committee in 1972. Sir David welcomed Miss Derbyshire Olga Terenczyn, and Lady Huddie crowned June Barwick as Carnival Queen. Attendants were Sandra Hall, Susan Fisher, Annette Hawley, Carol Fern and Gillian Cooper.

WIRKSWORTH

Quick thinking by nine-year-old Andrew Taylor almost certainly saved the life of his young friend Neil Worth when he was trapped and sinking in sludge in a 17-feet deep filter bed. Andrew grabbed a nearby pole and called to him to hold it while he slowly dragged him back to safety. The pair were with Martin Worth and Andrew Waterhouse and all were playing at Wirksworth's Derby Road sewage works. Andrew, of King George Street, Wirksworth, received a severe ticking off for dirtying his clothes before his mother realised how brave he had been.

Matlock Bath's John Boden pictured disposing of Mike Kham in an early round of the Derbyshire junior and intermediate amateur wrestling championships at Wirksworth in 1971. Wirksworth AWC gained five firsts (Luke Hallows, Tony Phillips, David Wood, Victor Morley, John Boden) and Arthur Gratton, a second.

When it comes to sport Peter Lowe was a bit of an all-rounder. Although he considered himself only average – never having gained any County honours – he played soccer, rugby, tennis, billiards, snooker, bowls, badminton, darts and table tennis. In between he managed to relax by going fishing and cycling. Peter, of Cromford Road, Wirksworth, said he had a very understanding wife.

When Jack and May Smith were looking for somewhere to live in 1947 they found a house in Gorsey Bank, Wirksworth. It was the railway crossing keeper's house that went with the job of operating the gates and signals during the day as passengers and freight from the town quarries passed through. By 1974 only freight was moving and Mrs Smith, then widowed, was still carrying on with the work. At that time the job looked secure, but by 1979 and after 32 years in control of the crossing, it became automatic and for her it was the end of the line.

Lorraine Nicholl, Wirksworth's Well Dressing Queen checking weather prospects the day before 1974's festivities got under way. The 14-year-old's attendants were Yvonne Phillips and Janet Willis.

Looks like a busy day at the office for Peter Hodcroft ...but things are not as they seem. Along with his real-life wife Anne-Louise and Julia Ludlam they were taking part in Theatre Wirksworth's production of the comedy "Big Bad Mouse". Paul Wolfenden was producer and other cast members included Graham North, Anne Langhammer, Andrew Smith and Pauline Worthy.

Over fifty people were employed in the Wirksworth factory of fashion icon Janet Reger (above) – a name synonymous with underwear - when she closed her London premises and moved her operation to the town.

Poor old Santa – absolutely worn out after all those long hours spent delivering presents at Christmas. Wirksworth newsagent Harry Mitchell thought giving Santa a helping hand would be easy. It looks as if he was wrong.

With a total age of ten years between them Jane Ormond, Catherine Addison and Ruth Lownd almost brought the house down when they took to the stage and danced at Wirksworth Rotary Club's annual party for the town's senior citizens..

A big cup for little people – King George Street's version of Pinocchio at one of Wirksworth's spectacular carnivals.

Wirksworth Army Cadets were able to get a close look at two 105 mm guns when members of the 47 Field Regiment visited their HQ during a recruiting drive. Platoon Commander Mike Cheetham said the lads were thrilled to meet the Artillery men.

Former staff members of Wirksworth Maternity Hospital gathered in 1978 to honour Dr Leslie Fletcher who was about to retire after 49 years as a general practitioner in the town. He was presented by former Hospital Matron Miss J R H Southam with book and gift tokens while his wife Nessie received a floral arrangement, a Wedgewood bowl and chocolates.

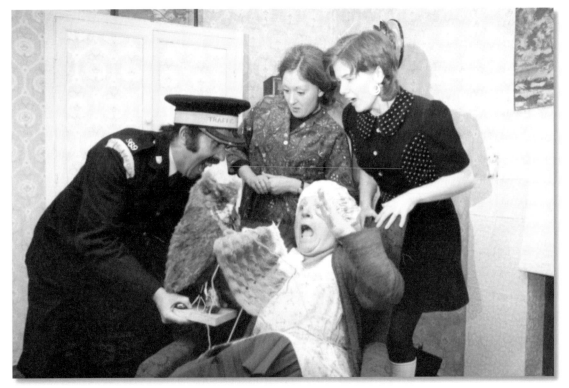

A traffic warden with a houseful of birds – both real and stuffed. That was the setting for "Just the Ticket", Theatre Wirksworth's production of John Waterhouse's comedy. Graham North was the traffic warden, his mother-in-law Pauline Worthy, his wife Julia Ludlam, their daughter Ann-Louise Hodcroft and her fiancé Peter Hodcroft. Ann Langhammer was producer.

The pitter-patter of rain failed to prevent the Duchess of Gloucester planting a magnolia tree in the garden at Alton Manor. She was protected by umbrellas held by (left) Lord Lieutenant Colonel Peter Hilton and Police Chief Superintendent Tom Bailey, Commandant of Buxton Division. The Duchess had stayed overnight with the Colonel and his wife Winifred at their home at Alton Manor.

With every muscle straining Matlock Cycling Club's Mark Hughes approaches the finishing line in the 1979 Burton and District Cycling Association's 25-mile championship. Mark, of Wirksworth, recorded his fastest-ever time of one hour three minutes and 18 seconds. Club mates Harry Gould returned in 1-5-40, Tim Gould (1-7-42) and John Hartland (1-7-46).

Malcolm Andrews celebrated his 18th birthday in memorable style – playing Billy on the opening night of Ivanhoe Theatre Group's production of "Billy Liar" at Wirksworth. Wendy Hepplewhite was the producer and her "team" included Wyn Saunders, Jack Hunt, Janet Dawson, Iain Mackay, Chrissie Garrett, Lorraine Wolsey and Jackie Price.

Even a petrol shortage and torrential rain failed to dampen enthusiasm at Wirksworth's Well Dressings in 1979. The crowning ceremony was moved into the Town Hall and Monday's Field Day was cancelled. BBC Radio Derby's Liz Swan crowned 16-year-old Elizabeth Gould as Queen watched by retiring Queen Helen Phair and attendants Carol Johnson, Julie Westerman, Claire Nowell, Alison Askey and page-boys David Martington and Michael Fern.

Wirksworth Well Dressings first prize winner in 1976 was wrecked by vandals who tore the clay from the images and threw it at nearby walls.

YOULGRAVE

All together now, girls, heave! These young ladies were all members of Youlgrave Junior Red Cross Group training under their leader Mrs Jan Wilson. They had been invited to take part in the 1971 Red Cross sports, which included tug of war, and Mrs Wilson, Bakewell Red Cross South Division Commander agreed to coach them. Youlgrave was well-known for its tug of war prowess, six men's national champion teams coming from the village. They were trained by "Nabbie" Oldfield who emigrated to Australia, but before he went he passed on many valuable tips to Mrs Wilson.

Simon Groom, BBC TV's Blue Peter presenter, and his Labrador Goldie, toured the area in 1979 collecting cheques for the programme's Cambodia appeal. Hope Valley College raised £1000, Youlgrave held a bring and buy raising £818, Lea School and Methodist Church members gave £231 while Stoney Middleton Primary School chipped in with £30.